PENGUINS

Printed in Hong Kong

97   98   99   00   01   5   4   3   2   1

Library of Congress Cataloging-in-Publication Data

Love, John A.
    Penguins / John Love.
        p.   cm. – (WorldLife library)
    Includes bibliographical references and index.
    ISBN 0-89658-339-2
    1. Penguins.   I. Title.   II. Series: Worldlife library.
QL696.S473L68   1997
598.47—dc21   96–48510
                                                                CIP

Published by Voyageur Press, Inc.
123 North Second Street, P.O. Box 338, Stillwater, MN 55082 U.S.A.
612-430-2210, fax 612-430-2211

Educators, fundraisers, premium and gift buyers, publicists, and marketing managers:
Looking for creative products and new sales ideas? Voyageur Press books are available at special
discounts when purchased in quantities, and special editions can be created to your
specifications. For details contact the marketing department.
800-888-9653

Photographs copyright © 1997 by:

Front cover © Kevin Schafer (NHPA)
Back cover © Rod Planck (NHPA)
Page 1 © Johnny Johnson (Bruce Coleman Ltd)
Page 4 © Johnny Johnson (Bruce Coleman Ltd)
Page 6 © Kevin Schafer (NHPA)
Page 9 © Doug Allan (Oxford Scientific Films)
Page 10 © Mike Potts (Planet Earth Pictures)
Page 13 © Gerald Cubitt (Bruce Coleman Ltd)
Page 14 © Johnny Johnson (Bruce Coleman Ltd)
Page 16 © Johnny Johnson (Bruce Coleman Ltd)
Page 17 © Johnny Johnson (Bruce Coleman Ltd)
Page 18 © Tui De Roy (Oxford Scientific Films)
Page 19 © Johnny Johnson (Bruce Coleman Ltd)
Page 20 © Eckart Pott (Bruce Coleman Ltd)
Page 22 © Ben Osborne (Oxford Scientific Films)
Page 24 © Peter Gasson (Planet Earth Pictures)
Page 25 © P V Tearle (Planet Earth Pictures)
Page 26 © Tui De Roy (Oxford Scientific Films)
Page 27 © Richard Coomber (Planet Earth Pictures)
Page 28 © Brendan Ryan (Planet Earth Pictures)
Page 30 © Daniel J Cox (Oxford Scientific Films)
Page 33 © Johnny Johnson (Bruce Coleman Ltd)
Page 34 © Jeff Foott (Bruce Coleman Ltd)

Page 35 © P V Tearle (Planet Earth Pictures)
Page 36 © Gunter Ziesler (Bruce Coleman Ltd)
Page 38 © Doug Allan (Oxford Scientific Films)
Page 41 © Allan G Potts (Bruce Coleman Ltd)
Page 42 © Luiz Claudio Marigo (Bruce Coleman Ltd)
Page 44 © Mike Tracey (Oxford Scientific Films)
Page 45 © Johnny Johnson (Bruce Coleman Ltd)
Page 46 © Rinie Van Meurs (Bruce Coleman Ltd)
Page 47 © Kathie Atkinson (Oxford Scientific Films)
Page 49 © Frans Lanting (Minden Pictures)
Page 50 © Frances Furlong (Oxford Scientific Films)
Page 53 © Kevin Schafer (NHPA)
Page 54 © Kevin Schafer (NHPA)
Page 57 © Hans Reinhard (Bruce Coleman Ltd)
Page 58 © B & C Alexander (NHPA)
Page 60 © Eckart Pott (Bruce Coleman Ltd)
Page 62 © B A Janes (NHPA)
Page 63 © Gerald Cubitt (Bruce Coleman Ltd)
Page 64 © B & C Alexander (NHPA)
Page 67 © B & C Alexander (NHPA)
Page 68 © Frans Lanting (Minden Pictures)
Page 69 © Kevin Schafer (NHPA)
Page 70 © A N T (NHPA)

PENGUINS

John Love

Voyageur Press

Contents

Discovery

Everyone knows what a penguin looks like. It is instantly recognizable because we have grown up with its engaging human-like image in countless children's books and cartoon characters, on TV commercials and advertizing. The penguin also gives its name to the most famous library of paperback books in the world, to a brand of chocolate biscuits popular in the United Kingdom and even to a Pittsburgh ice hockey team.

And yet the very first penguin encountered by Europeans was not a penguin at all. The first written account was by a man called Pankhurst who sailed across the Atlantic to Newfoundland in 1578. After the long and arduous voyage he put his crew ashore for fresh provisions. 'There are many other kinds of bird store', he wrote in his journal, 'especially at one island called Penguin where we may drive them ashore on a plank into our ship, as many as shall lode her.' These birds are also called Penguins and cannot fly.' These were not of course the birds we know today as penguins but Great Auks or Garefowl. They looked like a larger version of the Razorbill that still inhabits the coastal cliffs of Britain, but the Great Auk stood nearly 3 ft (1 m) high. Ornithologists gave it the scientific name *Pinguinus* though some now prefer to include it in the same genus as the Razorbill and Guillemot – *Alca*. Its second or specific name *impennis* implies how the Great Auk was flightless. Thus it proved easy prey for hungry sailors and 150 years ago it was rendered totally extinct.

The origin of the name 'penguin' is obscure but may derive from the Latin 'pinguis' or the Spanish 'pinguigo', referring to the large quantity of fat on the birds. So it was not surprising that when seamen ventured into the southern hemisphere and encountered large, fat, black and white birds unable to fly – just like Great Auks – they should call them penguins too.

King Penguins breed in huge colonies on the subantarctic islands.

Native peoples would have been familiar with these birds for thousands of years, and when Bartholomew Diaz first rounded the Cape of Good Hope at the southern tip of Africa in 1488 he must have come across penguins, but he left no account of them. It was Vasco da Gama, 11 years later, who described 'birds as big as ducks, but they cannot fly, because they have no feathers on the wings. These birds of whom we killed as many as we chose, are called Sotylicayros and they bray like asses.' Apparently 'sotilicario' was a Portuguese name for the Great Auk, but the birds that da Gama encountered were the species now known as Jackass, African, Black-footed or Cape Penguins.

In 1519 Ferdinand Magellan, en route to Asia round the southern tip of South America, stopped off at two islands near Cape Horn. He noted a great number of fat 'goslings' which could not fly and lived on fish. These we now know to have been Magellanic Penguins, closely related to the birds in southern Africa and sometimes also referred to as Jackass Penguins. (Here we shall use the term 'jackass penguins' (without a capital letter) to refer to all four *Spheniscus* penguins.)

As ships ventured further south looking for whales and seals, they encountered more species of penguins – some, on subantarctic islands, plain black and white or with curious yellow tufts on their heads, little blue penguins in Australia and New Zealand or, largest of all, the handsome Kings and Emperors. They would all have provided welcome additions to ships' hardtack and later came to be exploited for their oil and head plumes – but fortunately none were to go the same way as their original namesake, the Great Auk.

Cartoons often portray penguins in the company of polar bears but in reality the two never meet because penguins are confined to the southern hemisphere while the white bears occur in the northern. We also tend to associate penguins with snow and ice but only two species – the Adelie and the Emperor – actually live on the Antarctic continent. Another species – the Galapagos Penguin – lives at the Equator!

Gentoo Penguins have a circumpolar distribution but are not particularly numerous in any one location. Their nesting activity usually kills off the surrounding vegetation each season.

The Diversity of Penguins

The Maoris of New Zealand have a legend that Taroa the albatross and Tawaki the penguin were always bickering as to who was the better at flying and fishing. Eventually Tane Mahuta, the god of the forests and birds, settled the matter once and for all, offering them each a gift. To Taroa he gave the longest wing of any seabird so that he could sail the ocean winds far from land in search of food. To Tawaki he gave flipper-like wings, useless in the air but perfect for flying beneath the ocean waves where he could catch all the fish he needed.

Modern science has confirmed just how closely related are the albatrosses and the penguins. The two groups — the *Procellariiformes* and the *Sphenisciformes* — share numerous anatomical, physiological and behavioral features. The tiny chicks of Little Penguins even possess the tubular nostrils so typical of petrels and albatrosses. Biochemical studies also confirm this relationship and indicate how penguins are most closely related to the small diving petrels. The earliest fossils come from New Zealand, and indicate that recognizable penguins had diverged from a common ancestor 60 million years ago.

Penguins almost certainly derive from a flying ancestor, and a small one at that — probably similar in appearance to modern diving petrels or to the auks of the northern hemisphere. If a bird still wants to fly and yet use its wings for swimming underwater it must remain small. As the Great Auk testified, losing the power of flight allows birds to grow larger, limiting heat loss from the body and also enabling them to live in colder waters. Many fossil penguins approximate in size to the present-day Emperors of Antarctica — 4 ft (1.2 m) tall — while the largest stood 20 in (0.5 m) taller — almost up to a man's shoulder. One long-extinct giant appropriately named *Anthropornis* (the man bird) was found in Antarctica while another, rejoicing in the name *Pachydyptes ponderosus*, and

Like all penguins, these Rockhoppers must come ashore to breed and undergo their annual moult into a fresh plumage.

probably weighing a massive 176 lb (80 kg), came from New Zealand.

About 40 fossil species are known, nearly half of them from New Zealand. South America and Antarctica are almost as rich with a few more having been found in Australia and South Africa. This distribution, of course, closely mirrors the present day range of the *Sphenisciformes*. At one time these southern continents were all linked into one huge land mass known as Gondwanaland. When Africa and New Zealand split off some 50 million years ago penguins were already recognizable. By the time Australia and South America separated from Antarctica penguins of all shapes and sizes were flourishing — some even smaller than present day Little Penguins. Many of these archaic types had long, slender beaks for stabbing fish or grabbing them with a powerful, pincer-like action. However, about 20 million years ago, seals and smaller whales and dolphins appeared on the scene to compete with the penguins for food or even to prey upon them directly. Those *Sphenisciformes* that have survived to modern times tend to be smaller, with shorter, broader beaks for feeding on an assortment of smaller prey.

The number of species surviving in the world today can vary because some ornithologists prefer to recognize at least two species of Little Penguins; others consider the Royal Penguin to be the same as the Macaroni. At the moment the consensus is that there are 17 species. The Little, Fairy or Blue Penguins from Australia and New Zealand are considered to be the most primitive and classified alone in the genus *Eudyptula*. They are certainly the smallest — at little more than 2 lb (1 kg) in weight and standing 16 in (40 cm) tall — and have a fairly ordinary appearance, gray-blue above and white below. The Yellow-eyed Penguin, also from New Zealand and one of the taller species at 31 in (80 cm) and weighing 17½ lb (8 kg) occupies another genus *Megadyptes*. It has obvious links with the six crested penguins *Eudyptes* (4½-11 lb/2-5 kg). The Fiordland, Snares and Erect-crested are restricted to southwest New Zealand and its offshore islands, while the Royal is isolated on Macquarie Island

Snares Crested Penguins are confined to a single island group – from which they derive their name – to the south of New Zealand. They are closely related to Fiordland Crested Penguins.

Penguins rely on their stiff, paddle-like wings to swim, and use their powerful
feet and claws more for walking and resting on land. It is clear
why these particular penguins are called Rockhoppers.

in south Australian waters. Its close relative, the Macaroni – which has a black face – has a wider distribution in the subantarctic waters of the South Atlantic. The Rockhopper is even more widespread, diverging into three subspecies.

The four jackass penguins *Spheniscus* (4½-11 lb/2-5 kg) occur around South America (Magellanic, Humboldt and Galapagos) and off South Africa (Cape Penguin), and appear to be related to the Little Penguin. The two largest and most colorful – the King (35 lb, about 16 kg) and the Emperor (66 lb, about 30 kg) – form the genus *Aptenodytes*, each with a circumpolar distribution, the former in subantarctic waters and the latter on Antarctica itself. A more diverse trio, Chinstrap, Adelie and Gentoo at 9-15 lb (4-7 kg) make up the *Pygoscelis* group, sometimes referred to as brush-tailed penguins. With striking black and white markings Adelies and Chinstraps are quite widespread in polar waters. The Gentoo is much less numerous but extends much further north to form two distinct subspecies; those breeding nearest the Antarctic are smaller, with longer beaks, legs and flippers – a reversal of biological principles which state that polar animals tend to be larger with small appendages.

Adaptations

In 1620 Admiral Beaulieu considered penguins to be feathered fish and, in common with many fish, seals, whales and dolphins that share their marine environment, they have acquired a streamlined torpedo-like shape. Abandoning the power of flight, penguins no longer required a hollow, lightweight skeleton. Water is of course a denser medium than air so creatures moving through it need strong, sturdy bones for the attachment of powerful muscles. This in turn reduces buoyancy so less energy need be expended to stay underwater. The 'arm' consists of broad, flat bones fused at the wrist and elbow to form a highly efficient, fairly rigid paddle. When swimming underwater both upstroke and downstroke are powered, the flippers providing such manoeuvrability that a penguin is said to be able to reverse direction in only a quarter of its body length. A more cost-effective swimming technique can be employed over long distances and is known as 'porpoising', the bird leaping clear of the water at regular intervals to snatch a quick breath.

Occasional kicks can provide additional thrust but otherwise the stout little feet are only used as brakes and, of course, for walking or hopping on land; the short, sharp claws are useful for clinging to wet, slippery rocks. The comical waddling gait of penguins is one of their most endearing features and has contributed to their being credited with a human-like appearance. It was perhaps John Winter, sailing with Sir Francis Drake, who in 1578 first commented on the penguin's resemblance to humans: 'They walked so upright', he wrote, 'that a far off man would take them to be little children'. Early this century Edward Wilson took this analogy to its obvious conclusion mentioning the penguin 'in his

Emperor Penguins toboggan across the ice.

dress tail coat and white waistcoat' and the popular imagination has never looked back. When progressing over snow or ice penguins often find it easier to flop down on their belly and push with their feet – an action referred to as 'tobogganing'. The tail is made up of 14 or 16 stiff quills and serves as a rudder underwater and as a prop when resting ashore.

To dive underwater all warm-blooded creatures have to overcome three

Sleeping penguins, like this King, may still tuck their beaks under the
wing in the same way as their flying ancestors would have.

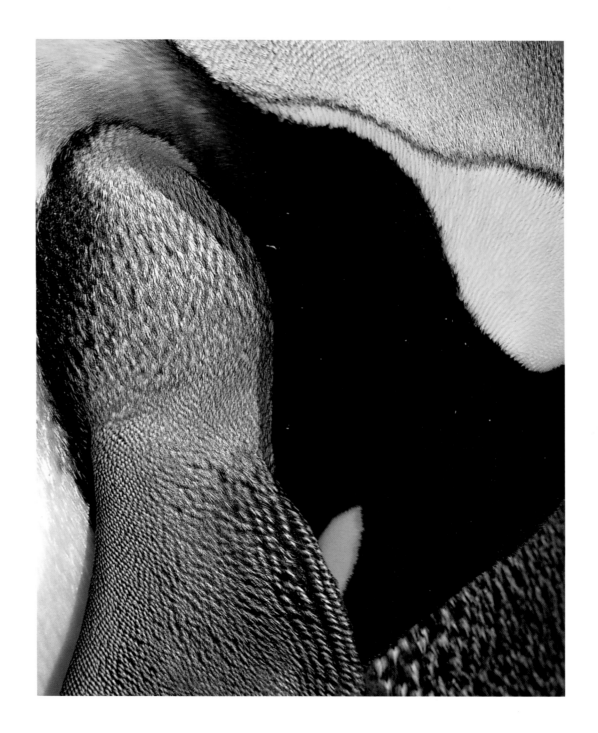

*Rather awkward on land, penguins come into their own at sea, effectively
flying underwater. King Penguins can reach depths of
300 ft (100 m) in search of fish and squid.*

problems: accessing enough oxygen to carry on body functions, withstanding pressure at depth and staying warm and dry. Haemoglobin in blood and myoglobin in muscles are complex proteins that display an affinity for oxygen, enabling it to be distributed around the body to nourish the tissues. Birds are no more remarkable than diving mammals but have an added advantage in that their lungs are not blind cul-de-sacs like those of mammals, but tubes that lead into capacious air sacs occupying any spare space within their bodies. Thus they enjoy a greater throughput of air. As a result, the amount of oxygen a Little Penguin can extract from each breath is in the order of 50%, compared with 30% in non-diving birds and only 15% in mammals.

Nearly a third of a diving penguin's oxygen requirement is carried in its lungs and air sacs, with another third or more in its blood and the remainder in its muscles.

King Penguins come ashore in surf.

It seems that penguins have only a limited capacity for extracting oxygen from myoglobin in their muscles before too many toxins build up. Thus they can only stay underwater for a maximum of 18 minutes, contrasting with an hour in seals. However, because of the efficiency of oxygen transfer through the lungs and air sacs, a penguin can get rid of toxins (especially carbon dioxide) very quickly and needs only a few seconds at the surface before the next dive.

Little Penguins tend to limit their activities to short, shallow dives. On the other hand Kings and Emperors regularly dive below 330 ft (100 m) and have

been known to reach depths of 1755 ft (535 m)! Normally, under pressure, gases are reduced in volume and dissolve into the blood. Four-fifths of air is of course nitrogen, which is of no value to the tissues but will come out of solution and form dangerous bubbles when the animal returns to the surface; in humans this is known as 'the bends' and can prove fatal. It is not fully understood just how penguins cope with this, but it seems particularly useful that more air is stored in air sacs where bubbles may form less readily than in the lungs. It is obvious however that penguins are better at diving than mathematical models derived from our current limited knowledge would predict!

A bird's plumage endows it with a waterproof and insulated coat. All diving birds have to keep their feathers in good trim, well anointed with a waxy, waterproof secretion, so they preen regularly and often. Rigid feathers can trap air which acts as insulation but might be forced out under pressure when penguins are diving at depth. Fat stored beneath the skin helps retain body heat and acts as a convenient food store, but it can inhibit movement, so penguins still rely on their plumage for up to 80% of their body insulation.

So effective are feathers in this respect that active penguins risk overheating, even in water, but especially when ashore in hot, sunny weather. Warm-weather species such as Cape and Galapagos Penguins tend to have relatively long flippers; here the feathers are shortest so excess body heat can be lost. Beaks and feet have no feather coat so also serve to radiate heat and several species from northerly latitudes have bare skin on their faces which flush pink to lose heat. Penguins from the lowest latitudes such as Emperors, have the longest feathers but the shortest beaks and flippers in order to minimize heat loss, and in cold conditions they will tuck their heads into the feathers and huddle together to conserve heat.

Breeding in huge numbers on the fringes of the Antarctic continent Chinstrap Penguins have also been referred to as Helmeted Penguins, for obvious reasons.

Feathers, Food and Feeding

The plumage of penguins is invariably dark, often black, above and white below, a coloration common to most diving birds. Thus they are less visible when seen from above against a dark sea or from below against a bright sea surface. Viewed from the side the effect is known as 'countershading'; the dark dorsal surface is highlighted while the light underside is in shadow so that the bird looks a more uniform gray and blends better into its background. All this makes penguins less visible to predators such as sharks, leopard seals, sealions and killer whales while also being less obvious to potential prey.

The four jackass penguins have conspicuous black and white stripes around the head and flanks. These are thought to confuse and concentrate shoals of fish when the penguins, often co-operating, swim round and round before picking them off one by one. Killer whales, with a similar black and white pattern on their flanks, are thought to use the same strategy.

Most of the diagnostic plumage features of penguins are concentrated around the head, a characteristic they share with other diving birds of the northern hemisphere, such as auks, loons and grebes. It has been suggested that swimming penguins, with only their heads visible, can thus recognize others of their own kind; but auks, loons and grebes lose this head ornamentation in winter. This idea may explain why Emperor Penguin chicks, which must huddle together to keep warm, have conspicuous white cheek patches when the young of most other species, even the closely related King, are uniformly dark or have only a light belly. On the other hand young penguins take several years to develop full adult plumage while the crests and head plumes tend to be sleeked down when wet and therefore not particularly visible at sea.

Head ornamentation also serves to enhance courtship and aggressive

Chinstrap Penguins roost together in large colonies on the ice surrounding Antarctica.

displays. Adelie Penguins twist their heads from side to side to display their white eye spots while Gentoo penguins, with white topknots, bow extra low. The crested penguins shake their tassels excitedly when displaying; if these are cut off they may experience difficulty in obtaining a mate – as was the case with King Penguins that had their orange cheek patches painted out.

It is also interesting that when two or more penguin species live alongside one another, they tend to have strikingly different head patterns – presumably to minimize the chances of interbreeding. Rockhoppers have different plumes from the other crested penguins, while Humboldts and Magellanics can also share colonies and are the most distinctive of the four jackass penguins.

Above: Humboldt Penguin.
Opposite: Macaroni Penguins, with their distinctive yellow crest, are named after eighteenth-century London playboys who had a passion for everything Italian and sported outrageous hairstyles.

The closely related Adelies, Gentoos and Chinstraps are the most divergent of all in appearance and can be found breeding together on several islands off the Antarctic Peninsula, but they avoid competing by differing in habits.

Both Adelies and Chinstraps feed largely upon tiny shrimps called krill that are abundant in polar waters. Chinstraps tend to take bigger krill but this may be because they breed a month later than the Adelies, by which time the shrimps are larger, more abundant and closer to land; thus they do not have to travel so far to forage. Gentoos tend to feed more in daytime when the krill retreat from the surface. Being larger than their two cousins, they can dive deeper and

This Galapagos Penguin's plumage demonstrates the effect of countershading. Light catches the dark back to blend better with the white belly in shadow, so rendering the bird less visible underwater to predator and prey alike.

by supplementing their diet with fish they find enough food close to the shore.

Rockhopper Penguins may be found alongside the slightly larger Erect-cresteds, Macaronis or Royals, but it is they who tend to be the krill specialists; the others taking more fish or squid. Less is known about the other crested penguins from New Zealand waters but it seems they too prefer crustaceans, such as krill, and even squid. Yellow-eyed Penguins on the other hand, take more fish while Little Penguins and all four jackass penguins take only fish. The latter range so far north because cold water currents provide rich upwellings of nutrients and plankton to sustain shoals of pilchards and anchovies. King Penguins feed almost entirely on larger fish, up to 4 in (10 cm) in length, but those breeding on Marion Island in the Australian subantarctic like generous helpings of squid. Emperors are more catholic in their tastes: some colonies subsist largely on fish, others take mostly squid and yet others mainly crustaceans.

Young King Penguins moult into their adult plumage.

All penguins are accomplished divers. Gentoos, for instance, have been recorded 650 ft (200 m) underwater, although usually their dives are not so deep and last only two or three minutes. Their foraging trips often total 90 dives in the space of four hours at sea. One bird however was recorded making 460 dives in 15 hours, resting no longer than 10 minutes between dives! Being the largest penguins it is not surprising to find that Kings and Emperors can dive the deepest and stay under for longest. Kings are known to swim up to

Cape Penguins enjoy the cooling ocean waves breaking over them on the coast of southern Africa.

1100 miles (1800 km) from their colony, diving to depths of 330 ft (100 m) and have been known to reach 1060 ft (323 m). Diving Emperors however often exceed 650 ft (200 m) and hold the depth record at no less than 1755 ft (535 m). An Emperor has been known to stay under for 18 minutes but this was probably exceptional. At the other extreme Little Penguins rarely go deeper than 16 ft (5 m), and are usually underwater for only a minute or so.

Moulting

The rigors of breeding, and constant preening, subject a bird's plumage to considerable wear and tear. Feathers must be replaced each year — usually after the nesting season. This moult takes place gradually over several weeks so that the bird retains sufficient feathering to keep warm. However, penguins lose their waterproofing so must stay ashore until the moult is complete.

For a bird like a King Penguin to produce over 2lb (1 kg) of new feathers can be quite demanding in terms of energy. It must therefore spend a few weeks at sea first, building up sufficient fat reserves to see it through the enforced fast of the moult. Indeed, penguins may double their weight, so the plumpest of them can find walking ashore rather awkward!

Little Penguins waste no time and replace their feathers within 18 days or so, while the larger Kings may take 32 days. Almost half of the body weight may have been lost in the process so the birds return to the sea forthwith, to recover condition before winter sets in.

King Penguins take nearly a year to complete their breeding cycle so find themselves having to moult just before they commence nesting again. Galapagos Penguins on the other hand live near tropical waters where fish stocks are notoriously unpredictable, so may breed less than annually. Thus they too usually have to moult just prior to breeding — a rare circumstance in any bird. In seasons when food is particularly scarce, however, these penguins have been known to skip nesting altogether rather than risk not moulting.

Penguin Society

It is all very well seeing penguins in zoos but nothing quite prepares you for the spectacle of a penguin rookery in the wild. I had seen a few hundred King Penguins breeding in the Falkland Islands but the colony in Lusitania Bay on Macquarie Island was incredible. Our ship emerged from the early morning drizzle in front of what I took to be a shingle beach. But a scan with binoculars revealed the 'stones' to be solid penguin. Tens of thousands stood shoulder to shoulder on every square foot of level ground. Hundreds more King Penguins sported all around the ship. We were told that 70,000 pairs nest here which, with non-breeders hanging around, may equate to nearly a quarter of a million birds altogether! The largest known colony however is in the Crozet Islands well south of Madagascar in the southernmost Indian ocean with an incredible 300,000 breeding pairs!

The South Sandwich Islands boast 5 million Chinstraps, half the world's population, and in complete contrast to the dozen or so pairs nesting at the Balleny Islands on the other side of Antarctica. Macquarie supports nearly a million pairs of Royal Penguins – a species found nowhere else in the world. From our boat we viewed hundreds of birds on rocks and skerries, standing like Lilliputians alongside two women researchers who had come down to speak to us. A little Royal played with the end of one of their bootlaces.

By contrast the four jackass species and Little Penguins usually nest in burrows so their rookeries may not appear so spectacular. Nonetheless a colony of Magellanic Penguins at Punta Tombo in Argentina comprises a quarter of a million pairs and presents an impressive cacophony of sound; rookeries I viewed in the Falklands were smaller in size. Some crested penguins nest deep under cover, in thick undergrowth if not in actual burrows. Indeed Snares

Normally sleek and trim, these King Penguins look slightly ragged
prior to moulting their old feathers and growing in new.

Crested Penguins have a talent for climbing over small trees to get to their nests. The smallest species – Little and Galapagos Penguins, together with Yellow-eyes – are the least social of all, pairs often preferring to keep out of sight of one another, voice playing an important part in social contact instead.

Penguin rookeries tend to be very traditional; on remote offshore islands good sites for a flightless bird can be hard to come by. Very few new colonies are ever established, mainly because mature penguins prefer to return to the colony of their birth. Here they are already familiar with the local geography and find safety in numbers, for a hungry leopard seal can only cope with one penguin at a time. Furthermore, by following the crowd a penguin is likely to be led to good feeding grounds. Finally, a large group of birds congregating at one spot for the summer is better able to synchronize its breeding activities, making it easier to find a mate for instance, or by swamping the ever-present skuas with eggs or chicks, thereby reducing overall predation.

Larger colonies may be safer and tend to produce more chicks per pair, 0.8 where only 50 Gentoos are nesting together compared with 1.18 in colonies of 300 pairs. Nests situated towards the centre of any colony also tend to enjoy a better breeding success than peripheral ones; they lay earlier, produce more two-egg clutches and may even boast a better hatching success. These factors tend to be a product of older birds being near the centre and younger, inexperienced birds on the periphery.

Displays

The most densely nesting species, such as Adelies and Chinstraps, possess a particularly rich repertoire of social signals. Nesting so far south, they have to compress their breeding cycle into the shortest possible time and have to be highly synchronized. They exhibit the most elaborate ecstatic displays, for

By following the crowd these King Penguins might be led to the best feeding grounds.

Mutual preening serves to reinforce the pair-bond. It may also be a comfort exercise, since burrow-nesting penguins such as Magellanics often suffer badly from fleas.

instance, to attract mates quickly. All penguins indulge in this behavior, spreading their flippers, stretching their necks skyward and calling loudly. Adelies, however, enhance this by vibrating their chests, clapping their bills and flapping their wings. Crested penguins shake their heads to flaunt their jaunty head plumes.

When a penguin wants to warn off an intruder, it waves its head from side to side, staring menacingly with wide eyes. The Adelie enhances the effect by bending its head to touch its shoulder. These intention movements are given as a warning to avoid an actual encounter but as a last resort the bird will lunge forward, peck or attack with beak and flippers. The mild-mannered Gentoo prefers merely to perform a ritualized gaping display to advertize its provocative orange gape. The most densely nesting species – such as Adelies, Rockhoppers and Macaronis – have an elaborate form of appeasement behavior to divert aggression; a bird attempts to look less conspicuous by compressing its plumage and less threatening by diverting its gaze. In Yellow-eyed Penguins this posture is aptly termed 'the sheepish look'. The Little Penguin bends forward to hide its white breast, an obvious target in the darkness of its burrow.

An irritable Macaroni Penguin.

Some Adelies and Macaronis have to move through 100 or more tightly packed neighbors to reach their own nests. This activity is made slightly less intimidating by the bird adopting the 'slender walk': moving rapidly through the throng on tiptoe, with head stretched high and wings spread.

Having attracted a mate, birds have then to confirm their tenancy of the

nest and to bond to one another by mutual displays, sometimes referred to as a 'welcome ceremony'. This is usually a form of the ecstatic display but performed in duet, for longer and with less head shaking (except in the case of the ostentatious Rockhopper of course). Bowing is a conspicuous feature in Gentoos, while a male Adelie initiates a bold frontal attack on its mate to induce her to bow submissively before they progress to full song. Eventually the display subsides into mutual preening. This habit is particularly well developed in Little and jackass penguins probably because, being burrow-nesters, they suffer from so many fleas and ticks anyway. Antarctic species do not seem to have so many parasites and rarely indulge in mutual preening.

King and Emperor Penguins do not defend territories so have incorporated many highly original elements to their displays. Huddling together to stave off the worst of the Antarctic winter, Emperors cannot afford to be too aggressive. For his ecstatic display the male sings with lowered head and once his mate appears the pair assume a face-to-face posture. In King Penguins this has developed to mutual sky-pointing, after which the pair duet together like an out-of-tune trumpet. Next they perform a 'waddling gait' through the colony, usually led off by the male. The distinctive swagger helps to keep the partners in contact with each other and to distinguish them from birds perambulating normally. This is followed by a bowing display and ultimately to copulation.

To mate the male penguin pushes from behind, touching the back of the female's head with his bill. If she is receptive she slumps to her belly so that he can mount. His flippers help maintain balance while their tails flick from side to side to make contact. King Penguins abandon the waddling gait after the egg is laid but, in the absence of a territory, duetting is still important to aid mutual recognition.

One of the most characteristic postures of penguins – including this Chinstrap – is the ecstatic display, designed to claim ownership of nesting territory and to attract a mate.

Nests and Breeding

King and Emperor Penguins are unique in that they have no need of a nest since they incubate their single egg on top of their feet. In all other species the nest is the focus of the breeding effort. If two or more species are nesting within the same colony they usually have distinct preferences in their choice of site to maintain contact with their own species yet reduce competition between species. Since Macaronis and Erect-crested Penguins breed earlier they seem to force the later Rockhoppers to steeper ground; in turn the presence of Kings can push the Macaronis to higher slopes. The rocky access routes to these higher colonies often develop deep scratches from generations of penguin claws to-ing and fro-ing.

On islands off the Antarctic Peninsula Gentoos tend to prefer flatter ground where their nests are generously spaced out – usually 40 in (100 cm) apart. Adelies, on the other hand, go for the windy knolls and ridges that clear of snow early in the season. With ice-free conditions at a premium the Adelies cram their nests only 30 in (77 cm) apart. Chinstraps can cope with the steeper and higher slopes where they nest at intermediate densities.

But even in these situations there is some competition. Adelies arrive a month earlier than Chinstraps and are sometimes forced to forsake their nest and eggs to their more aggressive cousins. Although the two species are the same size, the Adelies have already been fasting at the colony for several weeks while the Chinstraps are fresh and fit from the sea. Usually the Chinstraps have nested there in previous years while the Adelies tend to be young, inexperienced birds looking for their first nest site. Some Chinstraps become too enthusiastic, however, and one young bachelor tried nine different Adelie sites in his two-week stay at the colony. Chinstraps usually have to

Emperor Penguin chicks are hatched on the feet of the adult, under a warm and protective fold of belly skin.

resite these nests since they cannot tolerate being as close to neighbors as the Adelies. The Adelie's eggs are discarded but at least one pair of Chinstraps has been found inadvertently rearing an Adelie foster chick!

Most penguins construct only rudimentary nests but Adelies and Chinstraps can build a large structure of pebbles, probably serving to elevate the eggs above floodwater or mud. As Captain Scott's photographer Herbert Ponting observed, 'petty larceny is a common offence: penguins are habitual thieves and cannot resist the temptation to pilfer a stone from a neighbour's nest whenever a chance occurs'. His medical colleague, Dr Murray Levick, painted some pebbles red and placed them in a heap on a little knoll. Within hours they had all gone and he noted them being stolen from nest to nest all round his Adelie colony! He also saw pieces of tin and glass, half a stick of chocolate and the head of a metal teaspoon pilfered from the camp refuse heap to be incorporated into nests.

At the most southerly limit of their range Gentoos resort to using pebbles too and someone once took the trouble to count 1700 stones in one medium-sized nest. Gentoos generally prefer vegetation but soon destroy it by their nest building activity, trampling and guano. The ground may take several years to recover but the resultant growth is lush. Shepherds in the Falkland Islands appreciate this free fertilizer for their pastures. The Gentoos in the meantime move to a clean site 490 ft (150 m) away or more.

Fiordland, Snares Crested and Yellow-eyed Penguins also use stones, twigs and grass to line their crude nests which are usually placed in thick cover, overhung with roots, branches or grass or else placed in crevices and caves. Tending to nest at more temperate latitudes, these species need to protect their eggs from the sun and from potential predators. Galapagos and Humboldt Penguins seek dark, shady nooks and crannies while Little, Cape and Magellanics favor burrows, either appropriating them from other birds such as shearwaters or excavating them for themselves. These have a higher breeding success than

Some penguins are habitual thieves and cannot resist the temptation
to pilfer a stone from a neighbor's nest. This Gentoo
is no exception and may gather up
to 1700 stones for its nest.

*Nesting in more temperate latitudes, this Cape or African Penguin wisely
chooses to shade its clutch in a burrow. Galapagos Penguin eggs exposed to hot sun at
the tropics have been known to cook within minutes.*

nests placed out in the open, and the longer the burrow the more protected is the incubating adult or its chick from direct sun or wind.

So secretive are Galapagos Penguins that the very first nest, with two downy young, was not discovered until 1954. It was another six years before the first clutch of two eggs was found. Some nests might lack much shade and, in temperatures that may reach 104°F (40°C), one pair had to forsake their clutch around midday and resort to the sea to cool down; they returned to find that their eggs had cooked!

Eggs

Kings and Emperor Penguins lay only a single egg, necessitated by their method of incubation. Almost as soon as the egg is laid the male scoops it up from the female. He places it on top of his feet and covers it with a thick, warm fold of belly skin, which is richly endowed with blood vessels. Unlike Emperors, Kings are capable of laying a replacement egg if the first is lost. Birds are so desperate to fulfil their urge to incubate that if they lose their egg they will adopt almost any substitute – round pieces of ice, snowballs, stones, bottles, tins, a dead fish, even a leather camera case and a stale bun! Emperors have been seen to perform extraordinary feats of athleticism, even managing to scratch their head with one foot while balancing on the other and with the egg still safely tucked away in their abdominal pouch.

All other penguins lay two whitish eggs about four days apart. Young, inexperienced females may only manage one at first and some birds may lose an egg during incubation. Clutches of three have been recorded but are likely to be the product of more than one female or an egg rolling in from a neighboring nest. Cape Penguins can sometimes produce replacement clutches if their first breeding attempt fails, as do some Gentoos to the north of their range. But the Little Penguin is the only species that is regularly double-brooded, whenever a good season allows breeding to commence early.

The spread of laying tends to be compressed at southernmost latitudes where close synchrony is vital in such a restricted breeding season. With the exception of the Yellow-eye, incubation usually begins with the first egg so that this chick hatches out a couple of days in advance of its sibling. This gives it an immediate advantage so if food is short the second chick may starve.

Egg weight varies from 16 oz (450 g) in Emperors to 1.8 oz (50 g) in Little Penguins, 2-5% of the female's weight, smaller eggs in relative terms than almost any other bird. The two eggs are roughly similar in size in Little, jackass, Yellow-eyed and Chinstrap Penguins. In Adelie and Gentoo Penguins the first egg is from 2-5% larger than the second.

Adelie Penguins copulating.

In nearly all other birds where one egg is bigger, it is invariably the first to be laid. The crested penguins are unique, however, in producing a second egg that is larger than the first, sometimes by as much as 70%. Egg-swapping experiments have demonstrated how their first egg can still be viable. It may even hatch but only a single pair of Snares Cresteds and two pairs of Rockhoppers have ever been known successfully to fledge twins. Macaronis show the highest loss of first eggs, many before the second even appears. Having a tendency to incubate in a more upright position and to place the first egg to the front of the second, Macaronis tend to

As it nears fledging this Gentoo youngster will have to chase its parent
to verify its identity and win its meal of fish and krill soup.

Skuas are an ominous presence in every penguin colony. This one snatches an unattended egg from Gentoos. This can be an inevitable consequence of undue human disturbance.

lose it to predators like skuas. Few, if any, ever succeed in hatching both eggs. Other species have even been known to eject the first egg deliberately. At the opposite extreme, up to half of Fiordland pairs may hatch both eggs; only one chick survives but this is just as likely to come from the first egg as the second.

It is often claimed that the smaller egg is an insurance policy against losing the second egg, but this does not explain why it should be the first one that is the smaller. In addition, some species such as the Macaroni do not even keep the small first egg long enough to ensure against a later loss of the second. It is all very puzzling and promises to keep penguin biologists occupied for some time to come.

A Little or Fairy Penguin from Australasia.

Incubation

The 200,000 pairs of Emperor Penguins in the world are distributed amongst 35 colonies around the Antarctic continent where they demonstrate quite the most astonishing breeding cycle of any bird. As the Antarctic winter sets in – in March, or in some places a few weeks later – the Emperors, weighed down with fat, take up their stations on the sea ice. After a month or so of courtship the ice has set fast and the open sea is 60 miles (97 km) away. In early May the female lays her egg, leaves it with her mate and begins her trek back to sea; not having fed for several weeks she has lost a quarter of her body weight. Astonishingly the male remains at his post to see the egg through to hatching, enduring the worst that the Antarctic winter has to offer – winds often in excess of 125 mph (200 kmh) and temperatures as low as −140°F (−60°C).

All this time the males huddle tightly together to keep warm, backs to the wind and taking turns exposed on the outside. Each bird restricts his movements to save energy; one was known to stay on the exact same spot for 23 days! He even slows his body functions and metabolic rate and relies on his stores of fat to see him through. If he has misjudged he will have to abandon the egg. If all goes to plan the egg hatches after 64 days or so and the woefully thin father can still muster enough sustenance from the depths of his stomach to provide his offspring's first meal. Almost on cue, a few weeks after the sun has reappeared over the horizon, his partner returns, fat and sleek, holding 6.6 lb (3 kg) of fish in her crop to begin feeding the chick. The weary male needs no second bidding to relinquish it. He should still have a couple of kilos of food reserves to fuel the journey of maybe 100 miles (160 km) or so back to the sea to feed. He might have arrived at the colony four months ago weighing more than 80 lb (38 kg) but now departs at barely 44 lb (20 kg); any less and he will not survive to reach the sea.

Breeding much further north, King Penguin parents endure a less rigorous regime. By December, courtship is complete and egg-laying begins. This is a very protracted affair however and the very last eggs in the colony may not appear until April. The female leaves her mate to incubate and returns to the sea to feed. Eighteen days later she returns to take over, her mate having lost nearly a third of his body weight since he began courting six or eight weeks previously. He will return in another 18 days or so and the couple gradually reduce the length of their shifts until the egg hatches 54 days later.

Smaller penguins have shorter incubation periods, 35-38 days in most species and as short as 33 days in the Little Penguin. Yellow-eyed Penguins are unusual in being highly variable, pairs differing from 39 to as much as 51 days.

The male Emperor Penguin incubates an egg during the worst of the Antarctic winter, so that both parents can rear their chick in the short summer, when the sun never sets.

Although crested penguins lay two eggs, only one chick is ever reared to fledging – usually from the second, larger egg. Fiordland Penguins from New Zealand are both secretive and rare.

In all but the Emperor Penguin incubation is shared by both sexes, though the female may sometimes play the more major role.

Brooding chicks

A penguin chick takes a full day to break out of its shell; Kings and Emperors may take two or three days. Being covered with only a thin layer of down at first, the chick or chicks have to be brooded by the parents for several weeks until they are able to regulate their own body temperatures. In the Galapagos Penguin this brooding or 'guard phase' is more to shade the chick rather than to keep it warm. The period varies from two weeks in the Little Penguin, three weeks in most medium-sized penguins to six or seven weeks in Yellow-eyes, Kings and Emperors. Thereafter the chicks are left on their own for much of the time and both parents are free to forage at sea. The chicks may congregate into crêches, the size of which varies between species – from thousands in Kings and Emperors to only a few birds in Little Penguins, while other burrow-nesting species do not exhibit the habit at all. Crêches serve to reduce predation by skuas and giant petrels but in Emperor and King Penguins their main function is to enhance chick survival against the cold.

At first the chick will receive frequent small feeds each day but, nearing fledging, only one or two. Chicks recognize the call of their parent returning with food and are never fed by any other. Older Adelies sometimes have to pursue the adult through the colony, perhaps to reassure it that the most persistent chick is most likely to be its own! Adelies and Chinstraps, breeding during such a short Antarctic summer, have the fastest growth rate of all, their chicks fledging at 50-60 days and at only 80-90% of the adult weight. Most other species fledge at 60-80 days, but up to 100 days in Yellow-eyes and some Gentoos and Magellanics, even longer in Emperors and Kings.

Emperor Penguins have timed egg-laying for incubation to take place over winter so that the chicks hatch and grow during the short Antarctic summer.

A French scientist, Jean Rivolier, quipped how young Emperors 'regard their plump and weighty fathers as walking food cupboards, and they at once fasten on to them with the kind of blatant greed which only true hunger can excuse'! Time runs out, however, and after about 150 days the young fledge at only half of the normal adult weight, so starvation is a common cause of mortality, with of course the ever-present dangers from leopard seals and killer whales. Once the penguins reach breeding age – at about five or six years old – their survival prospects are reasonably good.

While the breeding cycle of Emperors on the ice shelf is remarkable enough, that of the King beggars belief. On hatching the chick is almost naked, dark gray and leathery, although its down grows in quickly. By the third week it is, according to biologist Bernard Stonehouse, 'grotesquely fat, pyramidal in shape and hung about with loose folds of skin'. At five or six weeks it is too big to shelter under the adult's belly and joins a crêche. After two months, covered in thick down, it approximates to the size of its parents. Early naturalists first thought these strange creatures a new species and named it the 'Woolly Penguin'.

By now winter is setting in and visits from the parents with food become less and less frequent and often stop altogether. From May until August – the most inclement time of year – a King Penguin chick, if it is lucky, may be fed only three times and the meals might be meagre. Many are not fed at all and the chicks have to live on their fat reserves. Like their cousins the Emperors they gain some insulation from their body fat and dense plumage but more and more come to rely on conserving as much energy as possible by slowing down metabolism, restricting all unnecessary movement and huddling tightly together against cold and storms. They stand to lose an incredible 70% of their body weight and if they were not at least 15 lb (7 kg) at the start of winter they will not survive. Thus many chicks of the late breeding Kings die.

Young Emperor Penguins have a distinctive white face, unlike the
plain brown woolly chicks of the Kings.

Towards the end of September the adults begin to resume their parental duties. The surviving chicks may weigh anything from 6½ lb (3 kg) to a comparatively 'healthy' 17½ lb (8 kg) and stand a good chance of fledging. After 24 weeks with little or no food they regain weight rapidly and by mid-November start to moult out of their down into immature plumage. It is amusing to watch them preening frantically, but there are still places that even a determined chick cannot reach. Some still sport a comical woolly cap when they finally take to the sea, their plumage otherwise a darker imitation of the adults.

Freed of their responsibilities, adults become obsessively itchy and themselves indulge in frenetic bouts of scratching until the colony becomes carpeted with moulted feathers. But it has taken them nearly a year to rear their single chick and they still have to moult, so it will be late summer before they are fit enough to court and ultimately lay an egg. They are, in fact, unlikely to succeed but, forced to break out of the cycle prematurely, they come into breeding condition early the following season. Thus, if they are experienced and lucky, they may manage to rear two chicks in the space of three years. The only other birds in the world that take longer than a year to reproduce are Wandering and Royal Albatrosses; they do not have the flexibility in laying dates so instead take a year out and only succeed in rearing one chick every two years.

Breeding success

Although most penguins produce two eggs per clutch few succeed in fledging both young, the average varying from 0.5-1.0 chicks per breeding pair. Kings and Emperors do well at 0.6-0.8 considering they only produce a single-egg clutch. Crested penguins effectively produce one viable egg but achieve only 0.3-0.5 chicks per pair. Yellow-eyes are amongst the most productive with 60% of broods being twins. Most other species can fledge twins – although

According to one scientist Emperor chicks regard their fathers as 'walking food cupboards'. This youngster is now too old to shelter under the duty parent.

the incidence can vary from year to year. Gentoos show greater annual variation than any other penguin and also demonstrate an increased productivity from north to south. Those on the Crozet Islands average only 0.5 chicks per pair while, near the Antarctic Peninsula when food is abundant, they can achieve 1.2, with one third of pairs fledging twins. It has also been shown how experienced Gentoos have double the fledging success of first-time breeders.

Lighter body weights amongst Magellanic Penguins were associated with late laying, smaller eggs and slow chick growth rates. This reflected seasons when fish shoals were either scarce or far from the colony. Lower fat reserves of breeding adults depleted sooner, forcing them to abandon eggs or chicks. In such poor seasons only 0.1 chicks might fledge per pair compared with 0.6 in good years. Galapagos pairs may average 1.3 chicks but without much food they can fail to breed at all. Humboldt and Cape Penguins also suffer, fluctuations in food abundance being a feature of their seasonal environment.

It is the rich upwellings of cold southern waters along the west coasts of South America and Africa that enable these species to exist so far into tropical climes. But every seven years or so the prevailing south-east trade winds falter allowing warm waters to move south. Fish stocks collapse and the effect on seabirds can be catastrophic. Sea breezes bring rain, often at Christmas time, so the Peruvian people have termed the event *El Niño*, the boy child.

Life cycle

Juvenile penguins are vulnerable to all sorts of dangers once they fledge and it is reckoned that half may die in their first few months at sea. During this time they may range far from the colony, one Little Penguin travelling 23 miles (37 km) in only three days and others being found up to 600 miles (966 km) away.

If they survive their first year or two at sea, the young birds begin to return to the colony. Out of 18,000 Adelies ringed in the Antarctic only 51 turned up elsewhere, most of them at another rookery less than a mile away.

Despite Macaroni Penguins rearing only one young per year, if they are lucky, they are the most numerous penguins in the world. No fewer than 11 million adult pairs inhabit the south polar ocean, together with countless more young, pre-breeders.

Indeed, so faithful are they to their natal colony that three quarters of them end up nesting within 656 ft (200 m) of where they themselves had hatched.

Like most other long-lived seabirds, penguins delay the onset of breeding. Gentoos, Yellow-eyes and Little Penguins, for instance, can breed in their second year, Kings and Emperors in their third and Macaronis and Royals not until they are five. Most individuals delay a few years longer; some Emperors may not breed until they are nine and one Yellow-eye male not until he was ten.

Young birds tend to arrive at the colony later than established breeders so are immediately disadvantaged in the quest for nest sites or mates. Furthermore they are often lighter in weight so may not have enough food reserves to see them through; they may need several seasons to perfect their courtship technique, or else they may change partners.

Older penguins can be more faithful to their mate – if both survive the winter. In some species, and in good years, 90% of pairs remain together, often over many years (13 in the case of two Yellow-eyes). Adelies, with such a short summer, cannot afford to hang around for too long so only 60% remain together from one season to the next. In Kings and Emperors this is even lower, at 15-30%, probably because their breeding strategy gives such minimal contact with each other that they fail to form strong bonds.

Lance Richdale's classic study of Yellow-eyed Penguins revealed how two-year-old females tended to lay later, produced more single-egg clutches and laid smaller then average eggs, of which only a third hatched. Nearly all mature females laid two eggs, however, of which 92% hatched. Very old birds (13 or over) still breeding produced the smallest eggs, of which only 77% hatched.

Although a captive Emperor has lived to be 34, few wild penguins could expect to reach such a ripe old age. Having said that, a Little Penguin reached 21 and the oldest Yellow-eye in the wild is 23.

Chinstrap Penguins gather in the surreal setting of a blue iceberg.

Conservation

Global climate can have a considerable impact on penguin populations. During *El Niño* in 1973 no Galapagos Penguins bred. In 1982-83 the population crashed by 77% to only 400 individuals. Further events in 1983-84, 1987 and 1991-92 have slowed recovery and a census in 1995 revealed only 844, giving the Galapagos the dubious distinction of being the world's rarest penguin.

Recent surveys indicate that the Fiordland Penguin may now number fewer than 1000 pairs. The colonies of this secretive little crested penguin around the southwest shores of New Zealand are often inaccessible and hidden in dense undergrowth, making an accurate census difficult. The reason for its marked decline this century is unknown although dogs, rats and wekas all prey upon eggs and chicks.

Not much more abundant is the Yellow-eyed Penguin, with some 1500 pairs, half of them in the Auckland Islands, others on Campbell and Stewart Islands and only 300 or so pairs on mainland New Zealand. While food supplies might be affecting the southern populations, on the mainland the dangers are mainly man-induced. The population has declined by at least 75% in the last 40 years. Initially, the reason was human disturbance at the breeding sites and the clearing of forests for farming. Cattle trample nests and adult penguins are caught in fishing nets offshore, but more recently predation by introduced ferrets, stoats, feral cats and dogs have been the most significant causes of decline. Between 1988 and 1990 the population on the mainland decreased by 45%. In some areas 90% of chicks were being killed by stoats.

Nature reserves can and have been created for Yellow-eyed Penguins but this alone is not sufficient. There must also be suitable breeding habitat, so local volunteers have planted thousands of trees and shrubs to provide cover and

Denied the warmth of its parent's belly pouch this Emperor chick died. Had it grown a little older it would have benefited from its own body fat and warm down.

shelter for nests. Fences are also necessary, to exclude grazing animals so that the vegetation will regenerate. While it may be well nigh impossible to eradicate the predators completely, a trapping programme will reduce their numbers sufficiently to improve the survival of chicks and therefore boost the penguins' breeding success.

Changes in ocean temperatures, which in turn affect fish stocks – whether sparked off by global warming or not – may be the reason why Rockhopper Penguins have declined so dramatically. Their numbers around Campbell Island to the south of New Zealand are said to have fallen by over 90%. I was shown one once flourishing colony at Smoothwater Bay with now only a handful of birds. Another colony I visited on Sea Lion Island in the Falklands had declined from 150,000 pairs in 1932 to just 1000 pairs 50 years later. The problem is obviously widespread and does not seem related to any human-induced factor. It is conceivable that overfishing may have caused the Magellanics in the Falklands to become scarcer; on the other hand, the Gentoos there – one-third of the world population – seem to be almost holding their own. Furthermore, the Kings have recently recolonized and now number a few hundred.

The distinctive markings and crest of a Rockhopper Penguin.

Yellow-eyed Penguins, scarce in numbers, were the subject of a long-term study on mainland New Zealand by schoolmaster Lance Richdale. His work remains a classic of ecological research.

Adelies, together with the larger Emperors, are the only two penguin species found on the lonely continent of the Antarctic, somewhat at odds with popular belief. But even here they may not entirely escape the effects of humans.

King Penguins were wiped out in the Falklands by the turn of the century. It is said that the very last ones were boiled down by a shepherd to oil the roof of his house. They carry a layer of fat, almost an inch (2 cm) thick, under their skin which, rendered down in boilers, was used by sealers to top up their barrels of elephant seal oil. This industry reached its peak in the Falklands by 1860 when nearly three-quarters of a million penguins, mainly Kings and Rockhoppers, were being killed each year. I could still see the low, stone-walled corrals on West Point Island, where Rockhoppers were herded for slaughter.

Another industry came to be centred on Macquarie Island in 1891. At first Kings were the target but attention soon turned to the smaller, more numerous Royals, with some 150,000 birds being processed each year. By 1919 the island was declared a sanctuary and the penguins recovered their numbers. Now hundreds of thousands of Kings occupy the beaches of Lusitania Bay again, crowded round the rusted remains of the old boilers that wrought so much carnage not so long ago.

The inhabitants of Tristan da Cunha can be forgiven their use of penguin oil until paraffin became more readily available, and they supplemented their meagre income by selling curios made from Rockhopper scalps. The Falklanders too, harvested penguin eggs for the table. Gentoo eggs, with their rich red yolks, were special favorites, while Cape Penguins provided a similar harvest in South Africa. Between 1900 and 1930 over 13 million eggs were taken there and their collection only became illegal in 1969. These rookeries were also exploited for guano which was used as fertilizer, but it was the islands off Peru and Ecuador that provided the most prolific resource. 'Guano' is the Inca word for desiccated bird dung and in places, after hundreds of years with little rain, it had accumulated to depths of around 200 ft (60 m) – waste from millions of seabirds exploiting the rich anchoveta fisheries of the cold Peruvian current. Humboldt Penguins contributed to this export industry which once made up three-fifths of Peru's gross national product. The digging activities destroyed many Humboldt rookeries but it was the collapse of the local fishing industry that rendered this species the fourth rarest penguin in the world. Paradoxically Humboldts are one of the most commonly kept in captivity and might be the first encounter most people have with penguins.

Two other factors affect penguin populations, both products of this modern, technological age. The first is oil pollution. Magellanic and Cape Penguins nest around two of the most notorious sea passages in the world and there have been the inevitable catastrophes with oil tankers. With the closure of the Suez Canal in 1967 some 650 tankers a month had to be re-routed round the perilous waters of the Cape of Good Hope. Eleven tanker incidents occurred in 1968 alone; in the worst, 15,000 tons of crude oil were released which led to the contamination of thousands of penguins. Spillages still occur with the resulting adverse effect on penguin populations, but over the years volunteers cleaning rescued birds have improved the survival rate considerably.

The second factor is eco-tourism. It has become a popular and profitable business to show people penguins in the wild. Visitors to Antarctica have increased from fewer than 300 per year in the 1950s to 6000 or more nowadays. From the engaging close encounters of the early Antarctic explorers, one tends to be lulled into the impression that penguins are very tolerant of human presence. Certainly some species seem to be and at a Volunteer Point in the Falklands I have had King Penguin chicks come up to me to tug at my bootlaces, or play with the straps of my camera bag. Gentoos are, however, more nervous and it is best to view colonies from the edge. Yellow-eyes and Fiordlands are even more nervous; the former are less inclined to land on a beach if there are people within 75 yards, for instance.

Some of the Yellow-eyed Penguin reserves on mainland New Zealand carefully direct visitors past the nests along paths screened by bushes or

About 150 pairs of King Penguins have now returned to the Falkland Islands to breed. Previously they were hounded to the brink of extinction for their oil.

Emperor Penguins cannot survive in isolation. To incubate during the rigors of the harsh Antarctic winter and to safeguard their chicks through summer snowstorms, there is security, safety and success in numbers.

fencing. But the most sophisticated example of visitor management is the Little Penguin colony on Phillip Island near Melbourne, Australia. The area is now a sanctuary, and predator control and speed restrictions on traffic have reduced the risks for the thousands of birds that come ashore, under cover of darkness, to their nests. The birds are even accustomed to the floodlights that improve the view for the 350,000 people that witness the spectacle every year – more than visit Ayres Rock in Australia.

Emperor Penguins with their young.

The huge Magellanic rookery at Punta Tombo in Argentina has increased in popularity, from only a handful of visitors 30 years ago to over 50,000 a year now, mostly concentrated where the birds nest most densely. Research has shown how Adelie Penguin hatching success is reduced by nearly 50% by visitor pressure, while even scientists themselves can lower it by a third; chick survival can also be affected.

Research is vital, however, if we are to understand penguin populations, while tourism can often be important to the economy of the small and remote human communities that live nearby. It is perfectly understandable that people should wish to see such endearing creatures at close quarters, and to study their fascinating habits. But penguins have enough to cope with in their natural environment without humans and modern technology compounding their problems unnecessarily. Let us hope that the future improves before any penguin species ends up like the Great Auk, that extinct 'penguin' of the opposite hemisphere.